Instant Bible Lessons for toddlers

God Takes Care of Me

Mary J. Davis

Rainbow Publishers

Rainbow Publishers • P.O. Box 261129 • San Diego, CA 92196

www.rainbowpublishers.com

To my inspiration for writing these books of Toddler Lessons, Caleb and Courtney.
Also, to big sister Shelbee.
Grandma loves you all.

And as always, to Larry.

INSTANT BIBLE LESSONS FOR TODDLERS: GOD TAKES CARE OF ME
©2004 by Rainbow Publishers, second printing
ISBN 1-58411-039-2
Rainbow reorder# RB38214
church and ministry/ministry resources/children's ministry

Rainbow Publishers
P.O. Box 261129
San Diego, CA 92196
www.rainbowpublishers.com

Interior Illustrator: Chuck Galey
Cover Illustrator: Mary Rojas

Scriptures are from the *Holy Bible: New International Version* (North American Edition), ©1973, 1978, 1984 by the International Bible Society. Used by permission of Zondervan Bible Publishers.

Printed in the United States of America

▪ ● ▪ Contents ▪ ● ▪

■ ● ■ Introduction ■ ● ■

Do your toddlers know that God takes care of them? Learning about God's care for His people is a first step to building a lifetime relationship with Him. After they participate in the activities in *God Takes Care of Me*, toddlers will know that God is involved in their daily lives. He took care of Noah, the Israelites, Elijah, Jonah, Daniel, Peter and Saul (Paul), and he will take care of us. Toddlers will learn to love and want to obey our loving God.

Each of the first eight chapters includes a Bible story, memory verse, and a variety of activities to help reinforce the truth in the lesson. An additional chapter contains miscellaneous projects that can be used anytime throughout the study, or at the end to review the lessons.

The most exciting aspect of *Instant Bible Lessons for Toddlers*, which includes, *Jesus Is My Friend*, *Growing Up for God* and *God Blesses Me*, is its flexibility. You can easily adapt these lessons to a Sunday school hour, a children's church service, a Wednesday night Bible study, or family home use. And because there is a variety of reproducible ideas from which to choose (see below), you will enjoy creating a class session that is best for your group of students, whether large or small, beginning or advanced, active or studious. The intriguing topics will keep your kids coming back for more, week after week.

Toddlers will learn that God takes care of us. They will begin to build a lifetime love of God.

✶ How to Use This Book ✶

Each chapter begins with a Bible story which you may read to your class in one of two levels, followed by discussion questions. Following each story page is a story visual for you to make and use as you tell the story. Every story chapter also includes a bulletin board poster with the memory verse and suggestions for using the poster as an activity. All of the activities are tagged with one of the icons below, so you can quickly flip through the chapter and select the projects you need. Simply cut off the teacher instructions on the pages and duplicate!

| craft | teacher help | story visual | action verse | bulletin board | activity |

| puzzle | coloring | song | game | snack |

• A Big Storm •

coloring

What You Need
- duplicated page
- crayons

What to Do
1. Hold up the picture so the children can see it as you tell the story.
2. Say, **God took care of Noah and his family. God will take care of us, too.**

Boom! The thunder made a loud noise. Courtney ran to Daddy.

Daddy helped Courtney climb onto his lap. "It's just a storm," Daddy said. "Soon, the rain will stop, and so will the loud thunder."

"I don't like the loud noise," Courtney said.

Daddy gave her a big hug. "God will take care of us during the storm," he said. "Do you remember the Bible story about Noah and his family in the big flood?"

Courtney nodded her head. She liked the story of how God took care of Noah's family and all the animals.

Daddy told the story again. "God told Noah to build a big boat. Then, God told Noah to put two of every animal on the ark. Noah and his family went inside the ark, too. Then, God made the rain come down for many days and nights. The whole earth was flooded. But Noah, his family and all the animals were safe inside the ark. When the flood went away, Noah and his family brought all the animals out of the ark. Noah thanked God for taking good care of them. God promised never to bring a terrible flood over the whole earth again. Then God made a beautiful rainbow in the sky to remind us of His promise."

Daddy pointed out the window. "Look at the sky. There's a rainbow. The storm is over."

Courtney looked at the rainbow in the sky. She smiled. God took care of her during the storm, just like he took care of Noah.

▪ Noah ▪

craft/snack

What You Need

- duplicated page
- graham crackers
- frosting
- animal crackers
- glue or tape

What to Do

1. Before class, cut out an ark for each child. Fold the ark on the dashed lines and tape the ends to form a box shape.
2. Give each child an ark, a graham cracker and some animal crackers.
3. Help the children spread some frosting on the graham cracker. Have the children stand some animals in the frosting.
4. Place the graham cracker inside the ark box. Say, **Noah gathered two of each animal and took them inside the ark.**
5. The children may eat some of the crackers as they work.

▪ Noah ▪

• Ark Snack •

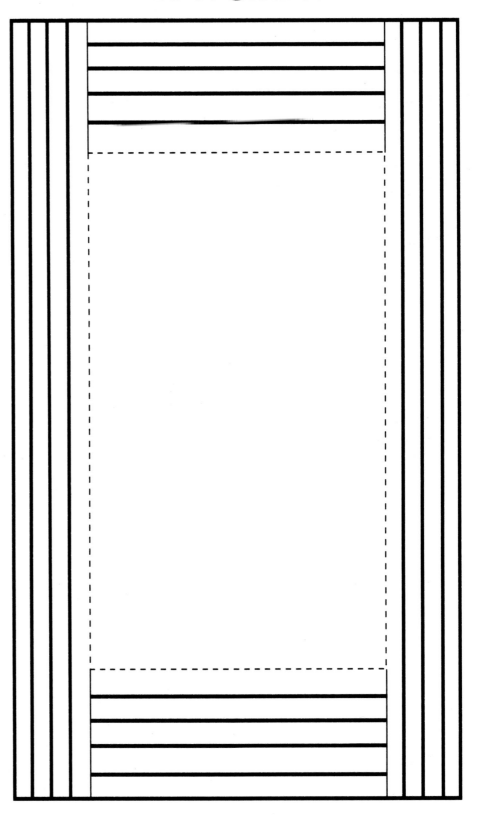

finished snack

• Gather the Animals •

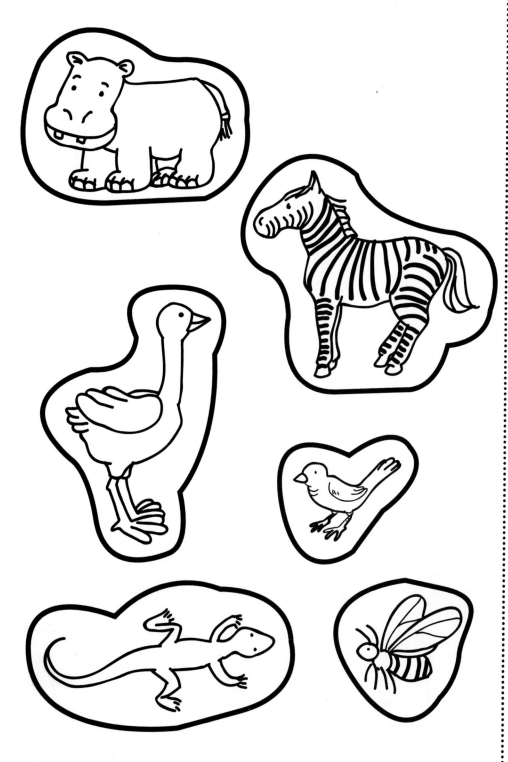

game

. . . .

What You Need
- duplicated page
- construction paper
- shoeboxes

What to Do
1. Before class, cut out the animals. Glue one of each animal on a separate sheet of construction paper.
2. Show the children the pictures of the animals.
3. Place the shoebox on the table.
4. While the children cover their eyes, place the animals around the room.
5. Have the children find all the animals and put them in the shoebox on the table.
6. Say, **God took care of the animals in the flood, and He will take care of you, too.**

▪ Noah ▪

17

Chapter 2

God Took Care of His People

Memory Verse

The Israelites went through the sea on dry ground. **Exodus 14:22**

* Story to Share *

2's and 3's ～➤

"Let my people go!" Moses told Pharaoh. God's people had been slaves for many years. Now God wanted His people to go free.

"No," Pharaoh said many times.

God sent 10 plagues on the people of Egypt. God made these bad things happen so Pharaoh would know that God was in charge, not Pharaoh. When Pharaoh finally got tired of the plagues, he said, "Leave! Go!" He was afraid of what else God might do. So God's people left Egypt.

"Oh, no," the people said to Moses. "How are we going to cross the Red Sea?"

"Don't worry," Moses said. "God has found a way to keep us safe. God will take care of us."

Moses stretched out his hand over the Red Sea. The water separated and made a path in the middle of the sea. God sent a wind and made the ground dry.

God's people crossed the Red Sea on dry ground! Everyone was safe. God took good care of His people.

1's and young 2's ～➤

"God says to let his people go!" Moses said to Pharaoh. God's people had been slaves for a long time. Now God wanted his people to be free.

"No!" said Pharaoh. But God made some bad things happen. Finally, Pharaoh said, "Go."

All of God's people left Egypt. But then they came to the Red Sea. "Don't worry," Moses said. "God has found a way to take care of us." Moses stretched out his arm. The sea waters moved and made a path. Then, God sent a wind to dry the ground.

God's people crossed the Red Sea on dry ground. God took care of his people.

Based on Exodus 5:1-2; 12:31-32; 13:17-14:31

Questions for Discussion

1. What did God want Pharaoh to do?

2. How did the people cross the Red Sea?

• Flip Booklet •

What You Need
- this page and page 20, duplicated
- two plastic or metal rings
- hole punch

What to Do
1. Cut out the four pictures on the solid lines.
2. Place the scenes in order.
3. Punch two holes at the top of each page, on the dots.
4. Place the rings through the holes to attach all of the pages together.
5. To tell story, hold the booklet so all the children can easily see the pictures. Flip the pages to the different scenes as you tell the story.
6. Say often, **God took care of His people.**

Another Idea
Let each child carry a stuffed animal or a backpack. Say, **We are leaving Egypt like God's people did. Let's walk a long way together. God took care of His people.**

■ His People ■

19

• Bulletin Board Poster •

bulletin board

. . . .

What You Need
- pattern on page 22
- construction paper or card stock
- clear, self-stick plastic
- glue
- sand

What to Do
1. Depending on how you want to use the poster (see ideas below and at left), enlarge, reduce or simply copy page 22 to fit your bulletin board space.
2. To use the poster as an in-class activity, duplicate the page for each child. Help the children spread glue on the "dry ground" path. Then allow them to sprinkle on some sand.

Poster Pointer

Copy the poster onto card stock for stability. Use colored card stock for effect. Attach the posters onto the wall at the children's eye level to use in review. Or, attach the posters to the wall outside your classroom so parents will be familiar with the lessons the children are learning.

■ His People ■

The Israelites went through the sea on dry ground.

Exodus 14:22

• Find a Way •

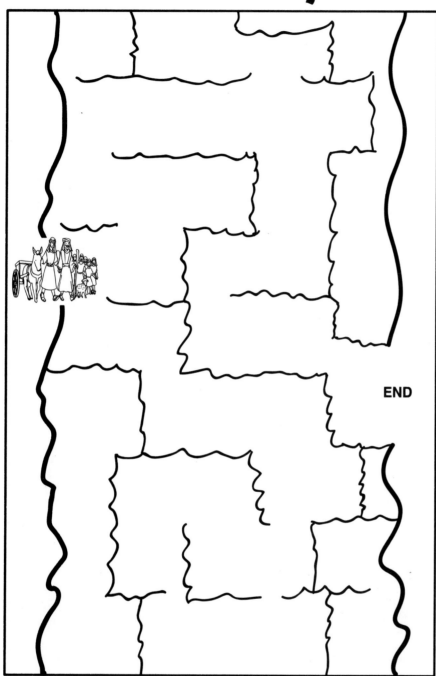

END

puzzle

What You Need
• duplicated page
• crayons

What to Do
1. Say, **Help the people find their way across the sea. Let's see which path goes all the way across the sea.**
2. Help the children follow the correct maze path.
3. While the children color the picture read the poem to them.

Let My People Go

God said, "Let my people go."
Pharaoh said, "No, no, no."
God sent plagues, there were ten.
Pharaoh said, "Don't do it again."

God's people started packing up
their stuff.
Then God said, "Go, that's enough."
They left Egypt very fast.
They were free, free at last.

They followed God's cloud in the day.
A pillar of fire at night led the way.
The people traveled far and wide,
Then stopped still by the Red Sea's side.

"What will we do?" they began to say.
Moses said, "God will find a way."
God moved the water from the ground.
And they crossed the Red Sea, safe and
sound.

■ His People ■

23

verse

● ● ● ● ● ● ● ● ● ●

What You Need

• duplicated page

What to Do

1. Teach the children the "God's People" action rhyme.
2. There are many actions to this rhyme, so try one verse at a time with the children. Then do another when they seem to understand what they are saying and doing.

God's people were slaves in Egypt. *hold wrists together*

But God wanted them to be free. *spread arms apart*

He told Pharaoh to let them go. *shake finger*

"If you don't, you'll answer to me." *point to God*

God sent some plagues to Pharaoh's land. *point outward to indicate lots of land*

Then Pharaoh said, "I've had enough." *clap hands together*

Pharaoh told Moses to take them away. *wave hands*

"Take all your people, their animals and stuff." *point toward "people"*

God's people were glad to be free. *make a smile*

They traveled all night and day. *pretend to walk*

They cried when they saw the big Red Sea. *pretend to cry*

Moses said, "God will find a way." *point toward God*

God told Moses to stretch out his arm. *stretch out arm*

And Moses stretched his arm wide. *stretch arm more*

The sea waters parted, the ground was dried. *pretend to step into the path*

God took them safely to the other side. *pretend to walk*

■ His People ■

• Match and Place •

What You Need
- duplicated page
- crayons

What to Do
1. Before class, cut out the puzzle square and the three figures.
2. While the children color the puzzle and the figures, say, **This is a picture of the people crossing the Red Sea. God took care of His people.**
3. Help the children match the three figures to the blank shapes on the puzzle.

■ His People ■

coloring

What You Need
- duplicated page
- crayons

What to Do
1. Hold the picture so the children can see it as you tell the story.
2. Let the children color the picture to take home.
3. Say, **God will take care of us.**

• God Makes a Way •

Mommy and Maria put the last of the frosting on the cake.

"I am so glad that Grandpa is coming to visit," Mommy said.

Maria clapped her sticky hands together. "I love it when Grandpa comes to see us. I'm glad we prayed for him."

Mommy smiled. "Yes, Grandpa was very worried his car wouldn't make it all this way."

"But God helped Grandpa find a way," Maria said. "Now Grandpa is coming on the bus."

"Yes." Mommy patted Maria's head. "A friend gave Grandpa some money to buy a ticket on the bus. Now Grandpa is coming to see us."

"God made a way," Maria sang to a tune she made up. "God made a way. Grandpa wanted to come and visit. So God made a way."

• Lunch to Go •

The Israelites went through
the sea on dry ground.
Exodus 14:22

What You Need
- duplicated page
- plain paper
- tape
- dry snacks

What to Do
1. Before class, cut one 1" x 8" strip per child.
2. Help the children fold the page on the dashed lines and tape the sides together.
3. Show how to tape the paper strip to the front and back top of the basket to form a handle.
4. Let the children choose some of the snacks (ideas: pretzels, mini-marshmallows, cereal circles) to put in their baskets.
5. Say, **God's people took food with them when they left Egypt. God took care of His people.**
6. Sit together on a blanket and eat the snacks together.

■ His People ■

Chapter 3

God Took Care of Elijah

Memory Verse

The ravens brought him bread and meat. **1 Kings 17:6**

✳ Story to Share ✳

2's and 3's

God told Elijah a big secret. He said, "There will be no rain for a few years. It will not rain again until I make it rain. People will have trouble finding food and water.

"I want to take care of you. This is what I want you to do. Leave here and hide in the Kerith Ravine, east of the Jordan River. I will send ravens to feed you, and there is a brook with water for you to drink."

Elijah obeyed God. He went to the Kerith Ravine, east of the Jordan river. While he stayed there, God sent ravens to feed him. The ravens brought Elijah bread and meat in the morning. The ravens brought Elijah bread and meat in the evening. And, Elijah drank water from the brook.

God took care of Elijah.

1's and young 2's →

God told Elijah a secret. He said there wouldn't be any rain for a long, long, time. People won't be able to find food and water.

"I want to take care of you," God told Elijah.

God sent Elijah to a special place. There was a brook with water for Elijah to drink. God sent ravens to bring meat and bread to Elijah.

God took care of Elijah.

Based on 1 Kings 17:4-6

❓ Questions for Discussion

1. Where did Elijah get water to drink?
2. How did Elijah get food?

• Craft Stick Puppets •

craft

What You Need
- duplicated page
- two craft sticks (or straws)
- tape

What to Do
1. Cut out the scene and cut a slit at the line.
2. Cut out the two ravens and the Elijah figure.
3. Tape a craft stick to the back of each one.
4. To tell the story, start with the Elijah puppet. As God talks to Elijah, move him a little. Then take Elijah on a trip. Stand up the scene and insert the craft stick in the slit so that Elijah rests beside the brook. Fly the raven puppets back and forth to bring Elijah food.

Another Idea
Place rugs on the floor and play music. Have the children flap their arms and "fly" from rug to rug. Say, **God used the ravens to take care of Elijah.**

▪ Elijah ▪

bulletin board

....

What You Need

- pattern on page 31
- construction paper or card stock
- clear, self-stick plastic
- mini-marshmallows
- round cereal pieces
- towel

What to Do

1. Depending on how you want to use the poster (see ideas below and at right), enlarge, reduce or simply copy page 31 to fit your bulletin board space.
2. To use the poster as an in-class activity, make one copy. Provide mini marshmallows or round cereal pieces. Place this page on a table, with a clean towel under the picture. Have the children take turns tossing bits of food to Elijah on the picture. Praise their efforts. Say, **We are taking food to Elijah just like the ravens did. God took care of Elijah.**

■ **Elijah** ■

• Bulletin Board Poster •

Poster Pointer

Make the poster durable by covering it with clear, self-stick plastic. Let each child hold a covered poster. While the children are holding the posters, say the memory verse together several times.

The ravens brought bread and meat.
1 Kings 17:6

puzzle

What You Need
- duplicated page
- crayons

What to Do
1. Help the children find and circle the five ravens.
2. While they color their pictures, tell the story again or review the memory verse from page 28.

• Find the Ravens •

• Care Song and Rhyme •

God Took Care

God took care of Elijah,
God took care of Elijah,
God took care of Elijah,
He sent some bread and meat.

The birds carried food to Elijah,
The birds carried food to Elijah,
The birds carried food to Elijah,
They brought him bread and meat.

God Takes Care of You and Me

 point to God and self **God takes care of you and me.**

 *pretend to eat* **He gives us food like bread and meat.**

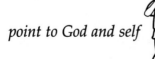 *point to God and self* **God takes care of you and me.**

 *fold hands in prayer* **Let's thank Him for good things to eat.**

song/verse

What You Need
• duplicated page

What to Do

1. Sing "God Took Care" to the tune of the "Bear Went Over the Mountain" two or three times so the children understand the words. To make an action song, point to God when He is mentioned in the first verse. Flap your arms for wings when the birds are mentioned in second verse.

2. Teach the children the "God Takes Care of You and Me" action rhyme. Do the actions slowly at first, so the children can mimic you.

■ **Elijah** ■

craft

. . . .

What You Need

- duplicated page
- black crayons
- glue
- tape
- construction paper

What to Do

1. Before class, cut out the hat and cut out the center of the hat on solid lines. Cut out the ravens. Cut paper into 1" x 6" strips. Have one hat, two ravens and one strip per child.
2. Allow the children to color the ravens. Place a hat on each child's head.
3. Glue a raven to the center of the strip. Tape the strip together at the back to form a bracelet. Place a bracelet on each child's wrist.
5. Use a loop of tape to fasten the remaining raven to the children's clothing as a badge.
6. Say, **God sent the ravens to feed Elijah. God took care of Elijah.**

▪ Elijah ▪

• Raven Wearables •

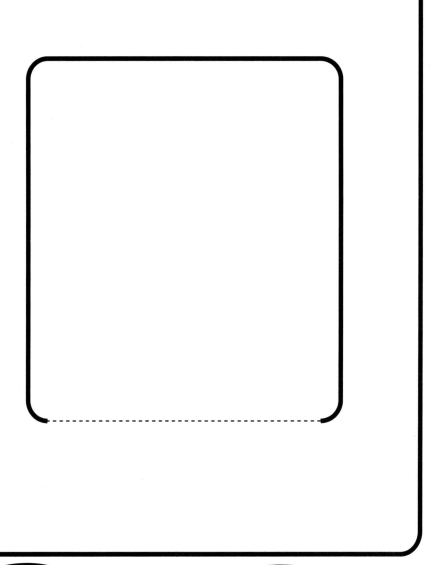

• God Takes Care of Julie •

coloring

What You Need
• duplicated page
• crayons

What to Do
1. Hold the picture so the children can see it as you read the rhyming story.
2. Allow the children to color the picture to take home.

"I forgot my lunch," Julie said.

The other preschoolers were eating their yummy sandwiches. Julie was hungry. She began to cry.

"Oh, my," the teacher said. "We must take care of Julie. Do you all remember the story of how God took care of Elijah? What did God send to bring him food?"

"Ravens!" Mark yelled.

"Ravens brought Elijah bread and meat," Keelie said.

The teacher smiled. "And what do you think God would want us to do about Julie's lunch?"

"We should give her some food." Mark said. "God can send us to help just like He sent the ravens."

Mark gave Julie part of his cheese sandwich. Keelie gave Julie two cookies. The other children shared, too.

God took care of Julie.

■ Elijah ■

craft

What You Need

- duplicated page
- construction paper
- paper plates
- crayons
- tape or stapler
- narrow ribbon pieces, about 8 to 10 inches long

What to Do

1. Before class, cut out the ravens and cut four 1" x 8" strips of construction paper for each child. Write on the center of the plates: "God sent ravens with food for Elijah."
2. Have the children color the ravens.
3. Evenly tape the four paper strips to the edge of a paper plate for each child.
4. Tape a raven section to the other end of each construction paper strip.
5. Poke two holes in the center of the plate and thread and tie a ribbon hanger.
6. Show how to turn the plate around until the ribbon is wound. Then have the children let go and watch it spin, making the ravens fly.

▪ Elijah ▪

• Flying Ravens Mobile •

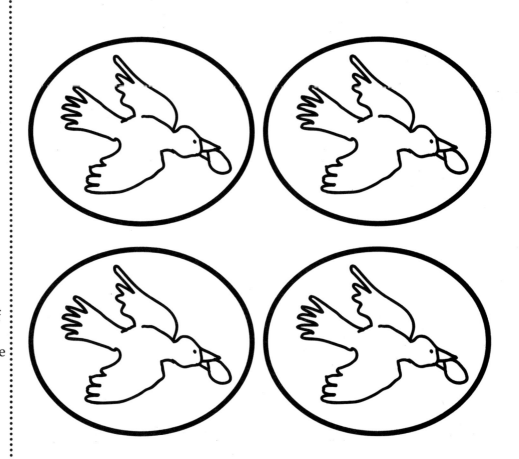

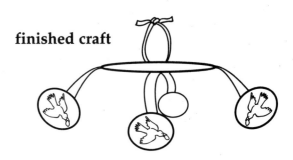

finished craft

What to Say

The ravens are flying to take food to Elijah. God took care of Elijah.

• Raven Server •

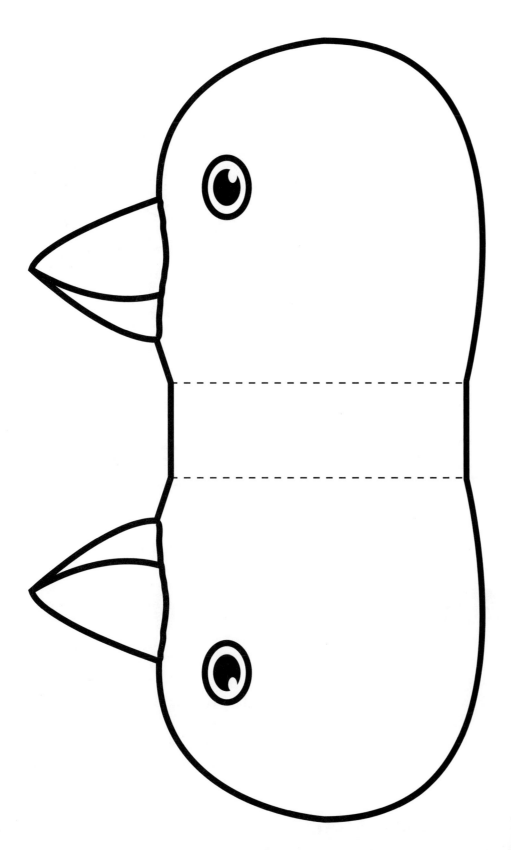

craft/snack

What You Need
- duplicated page
- pudding box
- tape
- soft bread

What to Do
1. Before class, cut out the raven head from the page. Fold the raven head on the dashed line. Cut bread into cubes.
2. Allow the children to color the raven head
3. Place the pudding box between the two sides of the raven head.
4. Make sure the open end of the box is facing upward. Tape the box into place.
5. Serve the children bread snacks using the raven server.
6. Say, **The ravens brought bread to Elijah. This raven is bringing you some bread, too.**
7. Serve water to drink. Say, **God told Elijah to stay beside the brook so he would have water to drink. God took care of Elijah.**

■ Elijah ■

Chapter 4

God Took Care of Jonah

Memory Verse

Jonah prayed to...God. **Jonah 2:1**

* Story to Share *

2's and 3's ⟿

God told Jonah to go to a city called Nineveh. But Jonah didn't want to go there. So instead, Jonah ran away! He got on a ship that was sailing far away.

But God already knew where Jonah was. He sent a big storm. The water came up over the sides of the ship. "We're going to crash!" yelled the men on the ship. Jonah was sound asleep in the bottom of the ship. The men woke him up and asked, "Why is this happening to us?"

Jonah knew why God sent the storm. "I ran away from God," he told the other men. "You need to throw me into the sea. Then God will take away the storm."

The men picked up Jonah and threw him into the sea. The storm stopped. God sent a big fish to swallow Jonah. Jonah was safe inside the fish for three days and three nights.

Jonah prayed and told God he was sorry. Jonah told God he would do what God asked him to do. He would go where God wanted him to go. Then the fish spat Jonah out, right on the shore. He was safe. God took care of Jonah.

1's and young 2's ⟿

Jonah didn't want to obey God so he ran away on a big boat.

But God knew where Jonah was. He sent a big storm. Wind blew the boat around, and water got inside the boat. The men were all afraid.

Jonah said, "I ran away from God. He won't take away the storm until you throw me into the sea."

The men threw Jonah into the sea. God sent a big fish to swallow Jonah. Jonah prayed inside the fish for three days and three nights. Then the fish spat out Jonah, right on the shore. Jonah was safe. God took care of Jonah.

Based on Jonah 1:1—2:10

❓ Questions for Discussion

1. What happened when Jonah was thrown into the sea?

2. What did Jonah do when he was inside the fish?

• Ribbon Story •

story visual

What You Need
- duplicated page
- construction paper
- ribbon
- tape
- glue

What to Do
1. Cut out the scene from the page. Glue the scene to a piece of construction paper for sturdiness.
2. Cut out the Jonah figure.
3. Tape a one-foot length of ribbon to the top of the scene where indicated. Tape the Jonah figure to the other end of the ribbon.
4. To tell the story, hold the scene so that all the children can see it. As you tell the story, move Jonah around to the various places (begin at the top of the page then move to the ship, sea, fish and land).

■ **Jonah** ■

bulletin board
. . . .

What You Need

- pattern on page 41
- construction paper or card stock
- clear, self-stick plastic
- glue
- crayons
- envelopes

What to Do

1. Depending on how you want to use the poster (see ideas below and at right), enlarge, reduce or simply copy page 41 to fit your bulletin board space.

2. To use the poster as an in-class activity, duplicate the page for each child. Glue the pictures to construction paper for sturdiness. Have the children color their pictures. Then cut the pictures into three or four simple shapes to make puzzles. Provide envelopes for the children to carry home the puzzles.

▪ Jonah ▪

• Bulletin Board Poster •

Poster Pointer

Copy the poster, then copy a letter to parents on the back with classroom updates such as the week's memory verse, a report on the child's good and bad behavior, supply needs and so on.

Jonah prayed to...God.

Jonah 2:1

puzzle

What You Need
• duplicated page
• crayons
• fish stickers

What to Do
1. Help the children follow Jonah's path to the boat, the fish and finally to Nineveh.
2. Read the story again on page 38 while the children work on the puzzle.
3. Give each child a fish sticker to place on the fish in the maze.

• Jonah Ran Away •

• Jonah Song •

Jonah

Jonah said, "I won't go."
"I won't go."
"I won't go."
Jonah said, "I won't go."
Then he ran away.

shake head

row boat

Jonah went away on a boat,
On a boat,
On a boat.
Jonah went away on a boat,
To run away from God.

God caused a great big storm,
Great big storm,
Great big storm.
God caused a great big storm.
The men on the boat were afraid.

make raindrops

throwing motion

Jonah said, "Throw me in the sea,
In the sea,
In the sea."
Jonah said, "Throw me in the sea."
When they did, the storm stopped still.

A big fish swallowed Jonah up,
Jonah up,
Jonah up.
A big fish swallowed Jonah up.
He was inside three days.

fish with hands

praying hands

Jonah prayed to God above,
God above,
God above.
Jonah prayed to God above.
The fish took him to the shore.

Jonah was kept safe by God,
Safe by God,
Safe by God.
Jonah was kept safe by God.
God took care of him.

hug arms

♪

song

· · · · · · · · ·

What You Need
• duplicated page

What to Do
1. Sing "Jonah" to the tune of "Mary Had Little Lamb." Sing slowly enough that the children can understand the words. Do the song at least twice.
2. After they learn the words, teach the actions

■ Jonah ■

coloring

What You Need
• duplicated page
• crayons

What to Do

1. Turn off most of the lights, so that the room is darker than normal. (Keep some lights on. Be sure to tell the children before you turn off the lights so you do not frighten them.)

2. Tell the story, then pray with the children. Say, **God, please keep each one safe, and help us to remember to pray when we are afraid.**

3. Give each child a copy of the page. While the children color their pictures, say, **Jonah was afraid inside the fish. Sometimes we are afraid. We can pray just like Jonah did. God likes when we pray. God will take care of us.**

■ **Jonah** ■

• Jared Prays •

Daddy turned out the light. "Good night," he said.

"I am afraid," Jared said. "I don't like the dark."

Daddy sat on the bed beside Jared. "See, I am right here with you, and you aren't afraid in the dark."

Jared scooted closer to Daddy. "But I don't like it when I am alone in the dark."

Daddy put Jared on his lap. Daddy folded his hands and prayed, "God, please keep Jared safe. Help Jared to not be afraid. Amen."

Jared folded his hands and prayed, too.

"I can go to sleep, now," Jared said. "I can pray to God. God will take care of me."

Daddy went out of the room. Jared prayed again. Then he fell asleep!

• Jonah Folding Book •

craft

God told the fish
to put Jonah on
the shore. God
took care of Jonah.

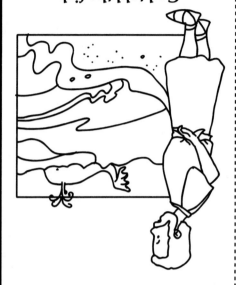

Jonah prayed
inside the fish.

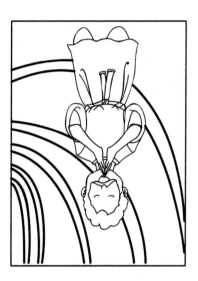

What You Need
- duplicated page
- crayons

What to Do
1. Before class, cut out the folding book for each child.
2. Help the children fold their pages on the folding lines to make the book.
3. While the children color their books, read the pages to them.
4. Say, **Jonah prayed when he was inside the fish. God kept Jonah safe and had the fish put him on land. We can pray to God, too. God takes care of us.**

I can pray to God.
God takes care of me.

Jonah Prayed

■ Jonah ■

craft

What You Need
• duplicated page
• tape

What to Do
1. Before class, cut out the two fish sections for each child.
2. Help the children tape the two fish sections together at the top.
3. Show how to look inside and find Jonah.
4. Read the verse to the children. Say, **God kept Jonah safe inside the fish for three days and three nights. Then God had the fish put Jonah safely on the shore. God took care of Jonah.**

• Where Is Jonah? •

■ Jonah ■

• Matching Fish •

game

What You Need
- duplicated page
- card stock, in five colors
- large bowl

What to Do
1. Before class, duplicate the fish on five different colors of card stock. Cut out the 20 fish. There should be four of five different colors.
2. Place one of each color of fish on the table. Place the remaining fish in the bowl.
3. Let the children take turns drawing out a fish.
4. Help the children place their fish on the matching colors of fish on the table.
5. Say, **Jeremy has a blue fish. Can you find where the blue fish goes? God sent a fish to take care of Jonah. God took good care of Jonah.**

■ Jonah ■

Chapter 5

Good Took Care of Daniel

Memory Verse

My God sent his angel. **Daniel 6:22**

* Story to Share *

2's and 3's ↝

King Darius put Daniel in charge of the kingdom. But others didn't want Daniel to rule over them! So they planned to make the king angry at Daniel.

"King Darius," they said. "You are so wonderful. Nobody should pray to anyone but you. If anyone breaks that rule, they should be thrown to the lions."

King Darius thought that was a great idea. But Daniel still prayed to God three times a day. When the men saw Daniel, they went to the king. "Daniel is breaking your rule!" they said. The king was sorry he had made the rule. He loved Daniel. Now he had to throw Daniel to the lions.

Early the next morning, the king rushed to the lions' den. "Daniel," he called. "Has your God rescued you from the lions?"

"Yes!" Daniel said. "My God sent an angel to shut the lions' mouths."

King Darius was very happy. He had his men take Daniel out of the lions' den. Then the king told all the people that God took care of Daniel.

1's and young 2's ↝

Daniel helped rule the kingdom. But some men were angry and they tricked the king. They told the king to make a rule that everyone could only pray to the king.

Daniel wouldn't pray to the king. He prayed three times a day to God. When the others saw Daniel praying, they told the king. Daniel was put in a place full of lions.

God sent an angel to care for Daniel. The angel shut the lions' mouths so they couldn't hurt Daniel. The king was glad Daniel didn't get hurt. He told all the people how God took care of Daniel.

Based on Luke 1:26-38; 2:1-7

Questions for Discussion

1. Where did the king put Daniel when he broke the rule?

2. Why didn't the lions hurt Daniel?

• Story Spools •

story visual
. . . .
What You Need
- this page and page 50, duplicated
- plastic gallon milk jug
- six thread spools
- tape

What to Do
1. Cut the milk jug to three inches from the bottom. Discard the top portion.
2. Cut out the six figures. Tape one figure to each of the six spools to stand up. (You can use blocks or plastic film canisters in place of the spools.)
3. To tell the story, begin with the milk jug bottom upside down to form a platform, as though it were Daniel's room. Place Daniel, praying, on the platform.
4. Stand the king and the men beside the milk jug bottom. Tell the story up to the point where Daniel is thrown to the lions.
5. Turn the platform upright, to create a "den." Let the
continued at left

What to Do, continued...

children see you placing the lions in the den. Move the king and men **figures to the outside of the den. Place the standing Daniel inside with the lions.**
6. **Move the king away from the den, but keep him on the table. Put the others away.**
7. Later, move the king toward the den as he and Daniel converse. Bring Daniel out of the lions' den when the story says he is removed from the den.
8. End by showing the praying Daniel. Say, **Daniel prayed three times a day.**

■ Daniel ■

• Bulletin Board Poster •

bulletin board

What You Need

- pattern on page 52
- construction paper or card stock
- clear, self-stick plastic
- glue
- yarn
- glitter

Poster Pointer

Copy the poster and tape several onto a table. Cover the table with removable clear plastic and provide crayons for a before class coloring activity. Wipe off crayon marks with a damp cloth after class to provide a clean surface for the following week.

What to Do

1. Depending on how you want to use the poster (see ideas below and at left), enlarge, reduce or simply copy page 52 to fit your bulletin board space.

2. To use the poster as an in-class activity, duplicate the page for each child. Help the children glue the page to a sheet of construction paper. Help the children glue 1-inch wide strips of paper around the edge of the picture to make a frame. Add a loop of yarn to hang. For older children, provide glitter they can add to the angel.

■ Daniel ■

My God sent his angel.

Daniel 6:22

• Dot-to-dot Daniel •

What You Need
- duplicated page
- crayons

What to Do
1. Help the children complete the dot-to-dot picture of Daniel in each scene.
2. Go to each scene and ask what Daniel is doing in each scene. Say, **Yes, he's praying to God. God took care of Daniel.**

■ **Daniel** ■

53

song

. . . .

What You Need
• duplicated page

What to Do
1. Sing "The Lions" to the tune of "Good Night Ladies," teaching the actions.
2. To calm the children for a story or prayer, sing "Daniel Prayed" with the children to the tune of "God Is So Good." Teach the actions as you go along.

• Daniel Prayed •

The Lions

Lions growled, *growl*
Lions growled,
Lions growled, *bite*
But they could not bite.

Angel stayed close, *cross arms on chest*
Angel stayed close,
Angel stayed close,
So lions could not bite. *bite*

Daniel prayed, *make praying hands*
Daniel prayed,
Daniel prayed, *bite*
And the lions did not bite.

Daniel Prayed

make praying hands

Daniel prayed to God.
Daniel prayed to God.
Daniel prayed to God,
Not to the king.

make a scared-faced look

In the lions' den.
In the lions' den.
In the lions' den.
Daniel was thrown.

An angel shut the lions' mouths.
An angel shut the lions' mouths.
An angel shut the lions' mouths.
And Daniel was saved.

touch mouth with hand

The king believed in God.
The king believed in God.
The king believed in God.
All the people believed, too.

 point to God

• Lion Snack •

snack

. . . .

What You Need
- bread
- round cookie cutters
- soft margarine
- shredded cheese
- raisins
- paper lunch sacks (optional)

What to Do
1. Help the children cut a circle from a piece of bread, using a round cookie cutter or the open end of a bowl or plastic glass.
2. Help the children spread margarine on the bread.
3. Show how to make lion faces by placing raisins for eyes, nose and mouth and shredded cheese around the edge for the lions' mane.
4. Give each child a paper sack if you are sending home the snacks.

■ Daniel ■

55

coloring

What You Need
• duplicated page
• crayons

What to Do
1. Hold the picture so all the children can see it as you tell the story.
2. Say, **We can pray anytime we want. God likes when we pray — even more than three times! God loves to hear us pray.**
3. Allow the children to color the picture.

• Three Times a Day •

"**L**et's eat!" Paige's brother, Timmy, said. He started to eat his breakfast.

"Wait!" Paige told him. "You forgot to pray."

"I pray before I go to bed," Timmy said.

Paige shook her head. "In our Sunday school story, we learned about Daniel," she said. "He prayed three times a day. Even when the king made a rule, Daniel prayed three times a day. Even when he was thrown to the lions, Daniel prayed three times a day."

Timmy nodded his head. "Okay, you're right. God wants us to pray more than once every day. Let's pray together before our breakfast."

Paige held her brother's hand and prayed.

▪ Daniel ▪

• Close the Lion's Mouth •

craft

What You Need
• duplicated page
• crayons

What to Do
1. Allow the children to color the picture.
2. Help them fold the page on the dashed lines.
3. Show how to hold the picture from the back to make the lion's mouth open and close.
4. Say, **God shut the lions' mouths so they couldn't hurt Daniel. God took care of Daniel.**

■ Daniel ■

57

craft

. . . .

What You Need
- duplicated page
- crayons
- tape

What to Do
1. Before class, cut out a praying hands for each child.
2. Give each child a praying hands.
3. While the children color the praying hands, say, **God likes it when we pray. Who can say when is a good time to pray? Yes, at dinner. Yes, at bedtime. Yes, even at playtime.**
4. When the children are finished coloring, attach a loop of tape on the back of their praying hands and stick the badge on their clothing.

■ **Daniel** ■

• Praying Hands Badge •

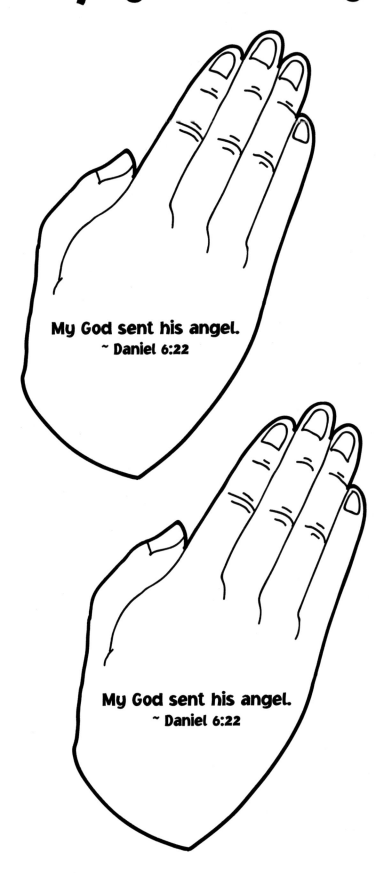

My God sent his angel.
~ Daniel 6:22

My God sent his angel.
~ Daniel 6:22

Chapter 6

God Took Care of Peter

Memory Verse

The Lord sent his angel and rescued me. **Acts 12:11**

* Story to Share *

2's and 3's ⟶

King Herod sent his soldiers to arrest Peter for preaching and teaching about Jesus. Peter was thrown into prison. He had chains on his arms, and many soldiers were guarding him. Two soldiers even slept next to Peter so that he could not get away.

The church prayed for Peter. All the people who gathered and learned about Jesus prayed that God would keep Peter safe.

Suddenly, in the night, an angel woke Peter. "Get dressed," the angel said. "Follow me."

Peter thought he was dreaming, but he followed the angel. They walked past soldiers, and then walked out the city gate. The gate opened all by itself!

Just as suddenly as he had appeared, the angel was gone.

Peter hurried to the house where the church was praying for him.

God took care of Peter. Peter thanked God. The church thanked God. God took care of Peter.

1's and young 2's ⟶

King Herod told his soldiers to throw Peter into prison because Peter told people about Jesus. The soldiers put chains on Peter. Many soldiers stayed by Peter so he couldn't run away.

Peter's friends in the church prayed to God. "Keep Peter safe," they prayed.

Suddenly, an angel appeared in the prison. "Get up," the angel told Peter. Peter's chains fell off his arms. Then Peter followed the angel out of the prison.

Peter went to tell the church that he was free. Peter thanked God. The church thanked God. God took care of Peter.

Based on Acts 12:1–18

Questions for Discussion

1. What did the church do when Peter was put in prison?

2. What happened to Peter's chains when the angel appeared?

story visual

. . . .

What You Need

- duplicated page
- coffee can
- tape

What to Do

1. Cover a coffee can with construction paper.
2. Color and cut out the three scene panels from the pattern page.
3. Tape the scene panels to the sides of the coffee can, evenly spaced around the can.
4. As you tell the Bible story, turn the can so the children can see each scene.

Another Idea

Make paper chains for the children. Tape 1" x 8" strips of construction paper into rings, looping each link to the previous one. Place a chain around the wrists of the children, as though they were chained. Let them break the chains or drop them to the floor. Say, **God sent an angel to help Peter. The chains fell off Peter's arms, and he went out of the prison. God took care of Peter.**

■ Peter ■

• Story Carousel •

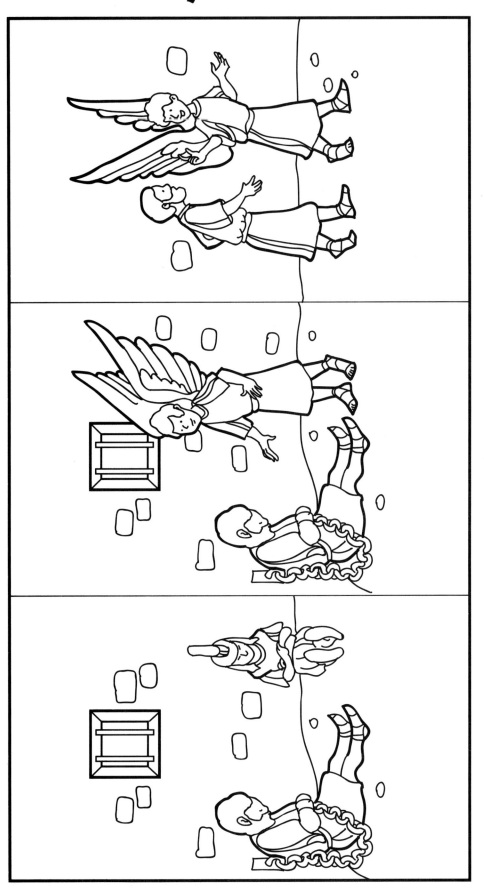

• Bulletin Board Poster •

bulletin board

What You Need
- pattern on page 62
- construction paper or card stock
- clear, self-stick plastic
- crayons

What to Do
1. Depending on how you want to use the poster (see ideas below and at left), enlarge, reduce or simply copy page 62 to fit your bulletin board space.
2. To use the poster as an in-class activity, duplicate the page for each child. Bend the angel section backward at the dashed line on your copy, so it is hidden. While the children color their pictures, retell the story. Then show the children how to make the angel appear and help Peter.

Poster Pointer

Copy each poster to card stock, one for each child. Punch holes in eight or 10 places around the edge of the card. Put a small piece of tape around the end of a one-yard length of yarn for easy lacing. Let the children lace the cards. Say the memory verse several times while the children are working and encourage them to say it with you.

■ Peter ■

The Lord sent an angel and rescued me.

Acts 12:11

• God Took Care of Me •

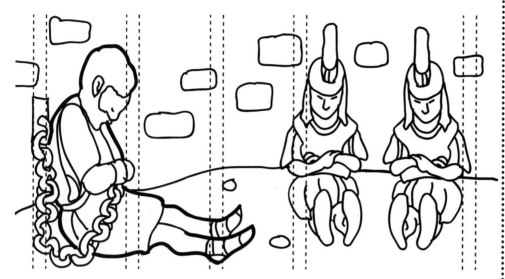

"**I** was thrown into prison by King Herod. He didn't want us to tell people about Jesus. Of course, I couldn't stop talking about all the wonderful things Jesus did. He's God's Son, you know. Who could stop talking about Jesus?

"Well, there I was in prison. Those heavy chains hurt my wrists. It was dark and smelly. There were soldiers all around me. Two soldiers had to stay by my side and sleep. King Herod did NOT want me to get away.

"I wasn't afraid, though. I knew all my church friends were together praying for me. They would stay up all night, praying.

"I must have fallen asleep. Suddenly, an angel touched me. There was a very shiny white light in my jail cell. I thought I was dreaming.

"'Quick, get up,' the angel told me. 'Get dressed and follow me.' So, I hurried to get dressed. I began to follow the angel. The soldiers in my cell were still sleeping. We walked right past some other soldiers. Then we came to the big gate. It opened all by itself. I was amazed.

"And there I was, standing outside the prison! We walked a little way, then the angel disappeared. I hurried to tell my friends that God had taken care of me.

"At first, they didn't believe it was really me. But then we all thanked God for helping me."

▪ Peter ▪

action verse

What You Need
• duplicated page

What to Do
1. Do the actions slowly as you say the "God Took Care of Peter" rhyme with the children.
2. Say the "Peter Was Freed" verse with the children. To add action to the verse, place your wrists together, then pull them apart quickly to indicate the chains being broken off.

• Free from Chains •

God Took Care of Peter

Peter was asleep in jail. *pretend to be asleep*

There was a soldier on each side.
touch each side of self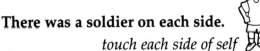

Then Peter heard an angel's voice

 *hand to ear*

And his eyes opened up wide.
open eyes wide

Peter's chains fell off his hands.

 shake wrists

The angel said, "Follow me."
beckon with hand

Peter was soon out of the jail.

His friends thanked God he was free. *wave hands*

praying hands

Peter Was Freed

Peter was in jail,

His hands were chained up tight.

God sent an angel

To help him in the night.

pull wrists together

Peter's chains fell off.

Angel said, "Follow me."

They walked right out of that jail.

And then Peter was free.

pull wrists apart quickly

• A Lost Mommy •

coloring

What You Need
- duplicated page
- crayons

What to Do
1. Hold the picture so the children can see it as you tell the story.
2. Afterward, allow the children to color and take home the picture.

"Stay close to me," Mommy said. "The store is crowded today."

Katie held on to Mommy's hand. There were lots of people around her, and it was very noisy.

"Oh, look!" Katie saw a big doll house. She pulled Mommy's hand. "Come on, let's go see it." Mommy's hand slipped from hers. Then, someone pushed her. Someone else pushed her the other way.

"Wait!" Katie yelled. "I can't find my mommy." But, it was too noisy. No one could hear her.

What will I do? she thought. Katie walked around the store, looking for her mommy. It seemed like a really long time, but she still couldn't find her mommy.

Katie felt like crying. Then she remembered Mommy told her God would always take care of her. Katie prayed, "God please help me find my mommy. She's lost."

"Can I help you?" a grown-up asked. "You look like you are lost."

"My mommy is lost," Katie said. "But I'm not supposed to talk to strangers."

"Stay right here," the grownup said. "I'll tell someone who works here."

Katie heard her name over the store intercom. "There's a little girl named Katie whose Mommy is lost. Will Mommy please come to the shoe department?"

Katie waited a little while. Then, she shouted, "Mommy!" because she saw her mommy coming down the aisle of the store.

Mommy hugged Katie. "I was looking all over for you. Were you afraid?"

Katie hugged Mommy back. "I was at first, but then I prayed. I knew God would take care of me. And He did!"

■ Peter ■

craft

What You Need
- duplicated page
- crayons

What to Do
1. Before class, cut out a pair of puppets for each child. Cut the holes at the bottom of the puppets.
2. While the children color their puppets, tell what each puppet is. Remind the children how the angel helped Peter get out of the prison.
3. Show the children how to put two fingers through the holes in each puppet and make them walk.
4. Say, **The angel said, "Follow me." Peter followed the angel right out of prison. God took care of Peter.**

• Peter Story Puppets •

• Make an Angel•

What You Need
- duplicated page
- paper towel tubes
- white paper coffee filters
- tape

What to Do
1. Before class, cut out an angel face for each child.
2. Give each child an angel face, a paper towel tube and a coffee filter.
3. Help the children tape the angel faces to the front of the towel tube, near the top.
4. Show how to fold the coffee filter in half and tape it to the back of the towel tube.
5. Say, **God sent an angel to help Peter get out of prison. God took care of Peter.**

finished craft

■ **Peter** ■

67

puzzle

What You Need

- duplicated page
- chocolate syrup
- shallow pan
- wash cloths

What to Do

1. Pour syrup into a shallow pan.
2. Help the children put their forefinger into the syrup, then press it onto the outlines in the picture. Wipe their fingers on a wash cloth when finished.
3. Say, **God sent an angel to help Peter. The angel told Peter, "Follow me." Peter followed the angel out of prison. God took care of Peter.**

• Fingerprint Maze •

Chapter 7

God Took Care of Saul (Paul)

Memory Verse

[They] lowered him in a basket.
Acts 9:25

* Story to Share *

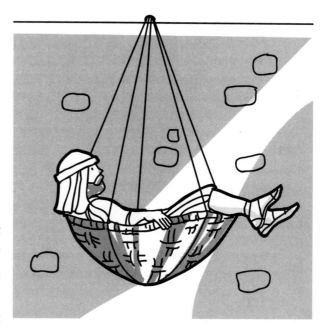

2's and 3's

Saul didn't like Christians. He didn't want people to teach about Jesus. But one day God changed Saul's life. Then, Saul began to tell others about Jesus.

This made the Jews angry. They didn't want Saul to talk about Jesus.

Saul heard that the men wanted to hurt him, so he needed to leave the city. But how? The Jews watched the city gates. They weren't going to let Saul get away safely.

But God had a plan. Late one night, Saul and his friends went to an opening in the city wall. They carried a basket with a very long rope.

"Get into the basket," the friends told Saul. Saul climbed into the basket. His friends carefully lowered the basket to the ground. Saul was safely outside the city. He went to Jerusalem.

God took care of Saul.

1's and young 2's

Saul didn't like for people to talk about Jesus. But one day God changed Saul's life.
The other Jews were angry with Saul. They wanted to hurt him. Saul needed to leave the city. God had a plan.

One night Saul and his friends went to a place where there was a hole in the city wall. His friends carried a large basket. "Get into the basket," they told Saul. His friends held tightly to the basket's rope and lowered Saul all the way to the ground. Saul got away from the men who wanted to hurt him.

God took care of Saul.

Based on Acts 9:1-25

? Questions for Discussion

1. Who changed Saul's life?
2. How did Saul get away from the men in the city?

story visual

What You Need

- this page and page 71, duplicated
- string

What to Do

1. Cut out the folding scene. Cut out the opening in the wall.
2. Fold the scene in half.
3. Cut out the folding figures from page 71. Fold each figure on the dashed lines.
4. Fold the basket on the dashed lines. The top and bottom sections will fold to the inside. When the center fold is made, these two sections will be hidden.
5. Tape a length of string to the basket.
6. To tell the story, stand the folding scene so the children can see the city. Use Saul as you tell how he was changed by God, and how the Jews were trying to find him. Move Saul around as though he is hiding inside the city. Then turn the scene to the wall section. Stand Saul's friends nearby, then *continued at right*

■ Saul ■

• Where Is Saul? •

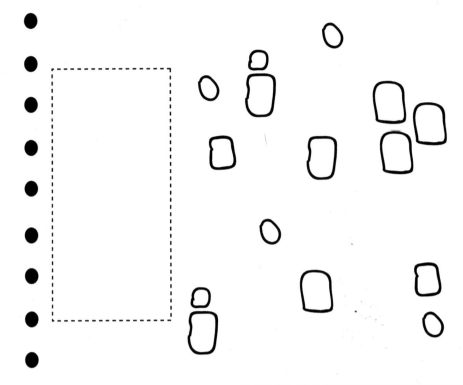

What to Do, continued...

move them behind the scene. Bring the basket up over the back of the scene, and slowly lower Saul to the ground. Open the basket to show where Saul was hiding.

• Bulletin Board Poster •

bulletin board

What You Need

- pattern on page 73
- construction paper or card stock
- clear, self-stick plastic
- paper grocery sacks
- glue

What to Do

1. Depending on how you want to use the poster (see ideas below and at right), enlarge, reduce or simply copy page 73 to fit your bulletin board space.
2. To use the poster as an in-class activity, duplicate the page for each child and provide small pieces of brown paper sack. Help the children glue the paper pieces onto the outside of the basket.

Poster Pointer

Make one or more copies of the unit poster book (see instructions on page 93). Keep the books visible for children to "read."

■ Saul ■

(They) lowered him in a basket.
Acts 9:25

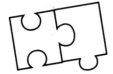

puzzle

What You Need
- duplicated page
- crayons

What to Do
1. Ask, **Where is Saul hiding? Can you find him? Draw a line around all the dots and see what is there.**
2. Help the children complete the dot-to-dot.
3. Read the verse to the children.
4. Say, **Saul hid in a basket. God took care of Saul.**

■ Saul ■

• Where Are You, Saul? •

Where are those Christians?
Saul looked far and wide.
But God made Saul change his mind.
Then Saul was on their side.

Where is that man Saul?
The Jews looked far and wide.
They were angry that Saul had changed.
So Saul had to hide.

What's in the basket?
Saul had a bumpy ride.
Friends lowered the basket down the wall,
And Saul was hiding inside.

• Saul in a Basket •

Saul in a Basket

A tisket, a tasket,

Saul hid in a basket.

The Jews watched the gates by night and day.

But Saul's friends helped him get away.

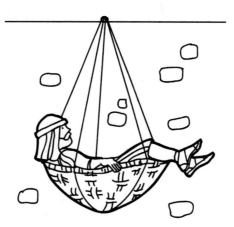

song

. . . .

What You Need
- duplicated page
- basket

What to Do
1. Show the basket while you sing "Saul in a Basket" with the children to the tune of "A-Tisket, A-Tasket."
2. Help the children learn the finger play to the tune of "Where Is Thumbkin."

Where Did Saul Go?

 hide hands behind back.

Where did Saul go? *bring out one hand and wiggle index finger*

Where did Saul go? *wiggle index finger again*

Here I am. *bring out other hand and wiggle index finger*

Here I am. *wiggle index finger again*

The Jews will never find me. *wiggle both fingers*

God is taking care of me. *wiggle both fingers*

Hide away. *hide one hand behind back*

Hide away. *hide other hand behind back*

■ Saul ■

75

craft

What You Need
- duplicated page
- crayons
- glue

What to Do
1. Before class, cut out the basket and Saul for each child.
2. Give each child a basket and a Saul figure.
3. Help the children fold the basket on the dashed line.
4. After the children color the basket and Saul, help them glue Saul inside the basket.
5. Repeat the memory verse.

• Make a Basket •

Acts 9:1-25

■ Saul ■

• Grandma's Lemonade •

coloring

What You Need
- duplicated page
- crayons

What to Do
1. Hold the picture so the children can see it as you tell the story.
2. Say, **God took care of Shelbee. God takes care of us.**

"I love to go camping," Grandpa said. "Let's get the tent set up."

Shelbee helped Grandpa set up the tent. She helped carry the sleeping bags inside the tent. Then Shelbee helped Grandma put the groceries on the picnic table.

"Let's make a fire," Shelbee said. "I'm hungry for hot dogs." Grandma, Grandpa and Shelbee cooked hot dogs and marshmallows over the fire. Shelbee ate her hot dog and lots of marshmallows.

Grandpa held his tummy. "Grandma always brings too much food. I ate too much. I drank too much of Grandma's good lemonade." He pointed to the many jugs of lemonade sitting on the table.

Suddenly, a big wind came. Sparks from the fire flew all around. Some grass caught on fire!

"I'm afraid," Shelbee cried. More and more grass began to burn.

"Don't worry," Grandma said. She tried to kick sand on the fire, but the flames got higher.

Grandpa said, "The pond is over that hill. I don't have any water." So instead, he grabbed the jugs of lemonade and poured them onto the fire. The fire died out.

"There," Grandpa said. "It's a good thing we had plenty of lemonade. Now I'm glad Grandma always brings too much!"

"God helped you think of pouring the lemonade on the fire," Grandma said. "God took care of us."

■ Saul ■

77

craft

What You Need

- duplicated page
- construction paper
- glue

What to Do

1. Before class, cut the four scene squares from the page for each child.
2. Help the children glue the scene squares in order on a sheet of construction paper.
3. Encourage the children to tell the story, using their story page.

• Glue-on Story •

1. Saul wanted to hurt Christians. Then, God changed Saul's life.

2. Saul began telling others about Jesus, God's Son. This made some of the Jews angry.

3. People wanted to hurt Saul because he was a Christian so his friends helped him leave in a basket.

4. Saul got away and went around telling people about Jesus.

■ Saul ■

Chapter 8

God Took Care of the Lost Sheep

Memory Verse

Rejoice...I have found my lost sheep.
Luke 15:6

* Story to Share *

2's and 3's

Did you ever lose something that you really loved? Did it make you sad? What did you do? Of course! You looked and looked until you found it.

Jesus told a story about how much God loves and takes care of each one of us.

"Pretend that you have a hundred sheep," Jesus said. "But one day when you count your sheep, you find that one is lost. You look and look until you find that sheep. You search everywhere.

"When you find your lost sheep, you would be very happy. You would say to everyone, 'Come and have a party with me. I am happy that I have found my lost sheep.'

"And that's how God feels about each person. He loves everyone so much and wants to take care of them. When a person comes to know God, all of heaven rejoices and is happy."

1's and young 2's

Did you ever lose one of your favorite toys or maybe a pet? When we lose something, we look and look until we find it.

Jesus told a story about how much God loves and cares for us. "If you had a hundred sheep," Jesus said, "and one was lost, you would look for it everywhere. You wouldn't stop hunting until you found your sheep. Then, you would be very happy and tell all your friends. You would say, 'Come see, I have found what I lost.'

"And that's how God feels about each one of you," Jesus said. "He loves you very much and wants to take care of you."

Based on Luke 15:3-7

Questions for Discussion

1. Who told a story about a lost sheep?

2. How does God feel when one of His lost sheep is found?

craft

What You Need
• duplicated page
• tape

What to Do
1. Cut out the two puppet sections.
2. Fold each section in half and tape it together.
3. Slip the Jesus puppet over your hand to tell the entire story. Slip the sheep puppet onto your other hand to tell about the lost sheep.

Another Idea
Make binoculars to help look for the lost sheep. Tape two bathroom tissue tubes together and cover them with construction paper. Let the children add stickers. Place pictures of sheep around the room and have the children use their binoculars to find them. (You can use any sheep patterns from this lesson to cut out and hide.)

■ Lost Sheep ■

• Hand Puppets •

• Bulletin Board Poster •

Rejoice...I have found my lost sheep.
Luke 15:6

What You Need

- pattern on page 82
- construction paper or card stock
- clear, self-stick plastic
- crayons

What to Do

1. Depending on how you want to use the poster (see ideas below and at left), enlarge, reduce or simply copy page 82 to fit your bulletin board space.

2. To use the poster as an in-class activity, duplicate a poster for each child. Cut on the solid lines around Jesus, keeping the dashed line intact. Fold the top part of the outline back at the dashed lines and stand up the picture. Help the children fold back their pictures after they have colored them.

■ Lost Sheep ■

Rejoice...I have found my lost sheep.
Luke 15:6

• Tracing Maze •

puzzle

What You Need
- duplicated page
- crayons

What to Do
1. Help the children trace the line from the shepherd to the sheep.
2. Retell the story from page 79 while they color their pictures.

■ Lost Sheep ■

83

song/verse

What You Need
• duplicated page

What to Do
1. Arrange the children in a circle. Hold hands and walk in a circle while singing "Where, Oh Where" to the tune of "Where Oh Where Has My Little Dog Gone?" Use each child's name.
2. Teach the "Look, Look" action verse to the children. Help them do the actions while you say the verse together.

• Look Where? •

Where, Oh Where

Where, oh where, has my lost sheep gone?

Where, oh where, can [name] be?

I've looked all over and he's [she's] still gone.

Where, oh where, can he [she] be?

Look, Look

Look, look  *hand above eyes to search*

The shepherd says. *touch mouth*

Look up high. *look up*

Look down low  *look down*

I love my sheep. 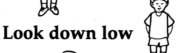 *cross hands over heart*

Look, look  *hand above eyes to search*

God says *touch mouth*

Look up high 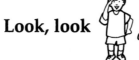 *look up*

Look down low *look down*

I love you. *cross hands over heart*

• Stuffed Bag Sheep •

What You Need
- duplicated page
- paper lunch sacks
- glue
- stapler
- cotton balls
- old newspapers

What to Do
1. Before class, cut out the sheep face and tail for each child.
2. Help the children glue the sheep's face to the closed end of the bag.
3. Show how to wad newsprint and stuff it inside the bag.
4. Staple the bag closed and glue the tail at the stapled end.
5. Help the children glue a few cotton balls to the outside of the bag.

finished craft

■ Lost Sheep ■

coloring

What You Need

- duplicated page
- crayons
- puppy stickers

What to Do

1. Give one copy of duplicated page to each child.
2. Read the story to the children while they color their pictures.
3. Let the children add some puppy stickers to their pictures.

• Wags Is Lost •

"Here, Wags!" Mommy, Daddy and Sarah yelled for Wags, their dog. He didn't come home.

"It's been all afternoon," Daddy said. "Wags has been gone a long time."

Sarah was sad. Wags was her very own puppy. "I love Wags," Sarah said.

Mommy went to the back door. "What is that noise?" she asked. Mommy opened the door. There was Wags!

"We're so happy you are home!" Sarah said.

Daddy picked up Wags. "You are just like the little lost sheep Jesus told about in the Bible. The shepherd looked and looked for his lost sheep. Then when he found the sheep, the shepherd was very happy. He loved his sheep."

Sarah remembered the story. "And God loves us just like that," she said. "God takes care of us."

■ Lost Sheep ■

• Sheep Necklace •

craft

What You Need
- duplicated page
- crayons
- tape
- crepe paper

What to Do
1. Before class, cut out the sheep pattern for each child.
2. Give each child a sheep. Have the children color their sheep.
3. Show how to tape the sheep to a length of crepe paper for a necklace.
4. Say, **God cares for us. Jesus told a story about a lost sheep to show how much God cares for us.**

■ **Lost Sheep** ■

craft/snack

What You Need
- duplicated page
- colored paper
- aerosol whipped cream
- wash cloths

What to Do
1. Duplicate the sheep on colored paper for each child.
2. Give each child a sheep picture. Wash each child's hands.
3. Squirt some whipped cream onto the pictures.
4. Let the children spread the whipped cream with their hands (allow for some licking of fingers).
5. Clean up with wash cloths when finished. The pictures can be thrown away when the project is finished.
6. Say, **What a nice job Stephanie is doing. Our story was about a lost sheep. God wants us to know he loves us, just like the shepherd loved his sheep.**

■ Lost Sheep ■

• Sweet Finger Painting •

Chapter 9

More Ways God Takes Care of Me

God Takes Care Song

Sing to the tune of "Farmer in the Dell"

Verse 1

God takes care of me.  *point to God then self*

God takes care of me.  *point to God then self*

It says so in the Bible. *hold hands together with palms up*

God takes care of me. *point to God then self*

Verse 2

God takes care of you.  *point to God then outward*

God takes care of you.  *point to God then outward*

It says so in the Bible. *hold hands together with palms up*

God takes care of you.  *point to God then outward*

craft

What You Need
- duplicated page
- card stock
- instant camera
- film
- yarn
- glue
- tape

What to Do
1. Duplicate the frame to card stock and cut out a frame for each child.
2. Take an instant photo of each child.
3. Help the children glue their photos to the frame.
4. Read the words on the frame to the children.
5. Tape a loop of yarn to the top of the frame for hanging.

■ More ■

• God Cares for Me

God Takes Care of Me

• A Growing Chart •

1

Noah

His People

What You Need
- this page and page 92, duplicated
- tape

What to Do
1. You can either use this idea for your classroom, or make one for each child to take home.
2. Cut out the chart sections. Section one goes at the top, then section two, then section three.
3. Place the chart 12 inches above the floor.
4. Use the chart throughout the theme lessons to show how tall each child is getting. Say, **John is getting so tall. God is taking care of John.** Even if the children do not grow significantly between lessons, they will enjoy backing up against the chart as well as the individual attention and affirmation you provide.

■ **More** ■

91

2   3

Elijah

Peter

Jonah

Saul

Daniel

His Sheep

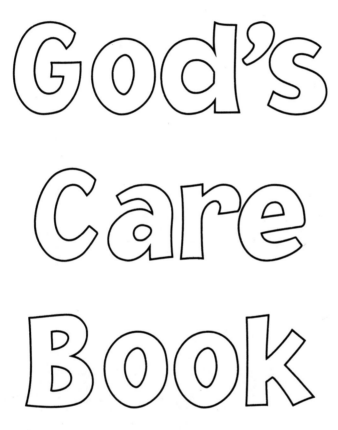

God's
Care
Book

craft

What You Need
- this page and pp. 11, 22, 31, 41, 52, 62, 73 and 82, duplicated
- construction paper
- glue
- stapler
- tape

What to Do
1. Give each child a copy of each of the eight bulletin board posters, plus this cover page.
2. Help the children glue each page to a sheet of construction paper.
3. Staple the left edge together to make a book. Cover the staples with tape to avoid injury.
4. Write each child's name on the cover page.
5. Allow the children to color the pictures and take the books home.

■ More ■

craft

What You Need
- duplicated page
- crayons

What to Do

1. Before class, cut out a flower picture for each child.

2. Give each child a flower picture. Help the children fold the picture on the dashed lines. Show how to make the pictures stand.

3. Say, **After you color your pretty flowers, you can give the picture to someone. Be sure to tell that person "God cares for you."** (For added enhancement to the lesson, take the children to a class of adults and have them give away their flowers.)

■ **More** ■

• Pop-up Flowers •

God Cares for You.

• Bible Story Mobile •

What You Need
- this page and page 96, duplicated
- string
- crayons
- tape

What to Do
1. Before class, cut out the nine mobile pieces for each child.
2. Help the children place four story figures on one length of string and tape them to the string.
3. Repeat with the remaining four story figures (order doesn't matter).
4. Tape the strings to the bottom of the Bible figure.
5. Add a loop of string to the Bible for a hanger. (For very young children, use crepe paper. It won't tangle easily, and it will be safer.)

■ More ■

95